Untalkable Love

Healing the Fracture that Makes Us Human

A Personal Manifesto

by Alec Tramposch

For Beth

There's a kind of a welcoming quality that you
associate with the highest form of civilization.
Because civilization, in a certain sense,
can be reduced to the word 'welcome.'

-- *Wynton Marsalis (2000)*

Untalkable Love

Clothes make the man. Naked people
have little or no influence on society.

-- *Mark Twain (d.1910)*

Untalkable Love

Part of me is alive. Part of me is not alive.

To be human, I need both.

Nature holds the answers to questions
we have not yet learned to ask.

-- *Kim Heacox (2009)*

Untalkable Love

1.

Since I can remember, I've asked the same question as so many among us: What the heck is going on with this "being-human" thing? Where did we come from, why are we here, where do we go when we're gone? While I didn't find a satisfying solution to my wonderings, I did come upon a few new and interesting questions that seemed to hold at least the possibility of some promising guidance:

> First I wondered why we humans are so much the same as nature – with feet and lungs and ears, while at the same time being so much different from nature – with libraries and automobiles and passports?

> Then I wondered why do we so often, for no seeming reason at all, feel alienated and isolated -- from the natural world, from other people, even from ourselves. Why is it so ding-dang hard just to be human day-by-day, when a squirrel or a lion seems to have no problem at all just being a squirrel or a lion?

> Is there a way, something we have longed for millennia, to heal this infuriating fracture, while still remaining human and connected to the civilized world that we know and love?

Several years ago, I left my 30-year career to seek some insight into these questions. What I found was as simple as it was unexpected. I learned that part of me is alive, part of me is not alive, and to be human I need both. And this unexpected insight led me to an even more unexpected, but simple and practical way to heal the fracture that makes us human.

Philosophers philosophize about everything
except civilization.

-- Albert Schweitzer
Philosophy of Civilization (1923)

2.

What I have learned is that human existence is a balance, an interwoven fabric, of what is alive in us and what is not alive in us. This balance is what makes us into civilized humans in the context of the natural world.

While there is no general agreement as to what we mean by a civilized human, there seem to be 3 levels of combination and balance of what's alive plus what's not alive in human existence:

> Civilization is a combination of living beings with instinctive vitality and natural needs, plus non-living institutions that are intended to meet those needs.

> Each institution is made up of living beings who agree to behave and cooperate according to a non-living set of rules toward achieving a common goal.

> Each individual human being is itself a mini-institution, made up of a Living Self, plus a set of personal rules and information which constitutes a non-living "institutional identity."

Gradually from naming an object we advance step by step
until we have traversed the vast distance
between our first stammered syllable
and the sweep of thought in a line of Shakespeare.

-- Helen Keller (1903)

3.

This interwoven fabric of what is alive and what is not alive in us is the result of our ability to talk to each other, using an unlimited number of words arranged according to the way the world itself works – the grammar of the natural world. Things are nouns, their characteristics are adjectives, their movement and change are verbs, and the things they change to or affect are objects. We adopted this grammar to talk about the natural world, but we use it cleverly to create new things that also have a stable existence.

One of the clever and stable things we learned to create through talking are sets of agreed rules for behavior and cooperation. We learned that nature has inherent rules, and that those rules have consequences. Once we had the ability to talk to each other, we ourselves could adopt agreed rules to enhance and replace many of the rules of nature. We even began to use agreed rules to decide how to make new rules, how to change them, and the consequences for breaking the rules.

Through these agreed rules and their enforcement we were able to achieve the complex and sustained cooperation that allowed us to meet our natural needs and further our individual and collective well-being better than we could do on our own in nature.

That is, they allowed us to create human civilization.

The chief thing demanded by
these intricacies of civilization
was control, restraint. A poise of self
that was as delicate as the fluttering of
gossamer wings and at the same time
as rigid as steel.

-- Jack London, White Fang (1906)

Untalkable Love

4.

It seems to me that civilization is uniquely human. We talk about animal societies, but I've never heard anyone talk about animal civilization. Yet it seems clear that living beings are the literal life blood of civilization and its institutions. Without living beings, civilization would be mere dust.

A blend of living beings plus agreed rules is necessary for civilization to exist, and a balance of the two, a balance of civilized instinct, is necessary for it to function. But only our living part has feelings, needs and a sense of well-being. The role of the non-living part is to serve the needs and well-being of the living part, and to channel our living vitality toward productive and cooperative behavior.

It might help to think about a horse in a corral. The horse is alive with natural and instinctive vitality. The corral is not alive, but it has a profound effect on the living being within it. Not to mention the reins and the saddle. These non-living parts restrict the horse's natural vitality, while at the same time providing discipline, protection, a place for nourishment, and the chance to serve us.

In the same way, the agreed rules of civilization that come from talking to each other constrain and discipline our natural vitality, in exchange for protection, nourishment and the chance to contribute to society.

The power of talking to each other to achieve complex and amazingly productive cooperation, and the futility of cooperating without being able to talk to each other, is beautifully told in the story of the Tower of Babel.

From the mountain forest, voices seemed calling.
I felt as dreaming, not my Living Self.

-- *Nez Perce warrior (1877)*

5.

So my first insight was this: the reason we humans are the same as nature while at the same time being different from nature, is at least in part because we are a balanced blend of what is alive and what is not alive.

As I came to understand it, the living part of me comes out of nature. It is born, it eats, sleeps, loves, thinks, talks, learns, works; it is creative, it has family, it has friends; it has ambitions, it has desires; it has talents and a personality. It is the part of me -- the only part of me -- that has feelings, natural needs, and a sense of personal and collective well-being.

My living self is much more than just my physical body, with all of its natural and instinctive abilities. It also includes my connections to other aspects of nature including other living beings from family to friends to coworkers to acquaintances. Any face-to-face encounter is living self to living self. My living self also includes my mind, my thinking, memory, imagination. It includes the skills I have learned, my natural talents, my very personality, and the experiences I have gathered during my life. It includes my ambitions, my intentions and my wisdom, as well as my insecurities and my doubts.

And, perhaps most important of all, it includes my feelings and natural needs, and my desire for a reliable sense of security and well-being.

Who am I, but a number on your list?
Who am I? No one's sure I exist.
Life today is hard, I'm just a face on a plastic card
I'm one of many numbers, not sure which one I am.

-- *Brian Lee and the Orbiters*
"Identity Theft" (2011)

6.

On the other hand, I came to realize that I also have a part of me that is not alive, a non-living identity that is created by our ability to talk to each other and establish agreed rules. It is made up of words and numbers, the rules-based information that I take on in order to interact with, to affect and be affected by, the institutions of civilization.

It includes my legal name and address, phone number, social security number, driver's license, nationality, educational degree, job title, property ownership, bank information, credit cards and credit score, political party, list of accomplishments, social position, even the style of clothes I wear. And much, much more.

I call this non-living part of me my "institutional identity," because it's what allows me to interact with the institutions of society, and with other people in their institutional roles. It is as essential to civilized human life as my natural living self, but its role is very different. The proper role of my institutional identity is to help me fill the natural needs and further the well-being of my living self and that of my close ones, by enabling me to accept the benefits of civilized institutions and contribute back to society.

A circus performer is the other half of a college professor. The perfect person has more than the professor's brain and a good deal of the performers legs.

-- Walt Whitman (1856)

7.

The reason that this strange system works so well is that, when all is said and done, both parts of me have the same goal: The well-being of my living self. The living part of me is the part that has feelings, needs and a sense of well-being. The proper role of my non-living rules-based institutional identity is to help fulfill these better than nature could do on her own. Our ability to talk to each other, to cooperate, and to come to agreed rules enables us to supplement and enhance the ability of nature to fill our needs and support our well-being.

For this extraordinary and elegant system to work, I myself have to be a kind of mini-institution, an individual living being that operates according to an accepted set of rules. In this way, I can interact with the larger institutions of society.

That the institutional identity is essential and inescapable is obvious to me. I couldn't do the simplest of civilized tasks — depositing or withdrawing money at a bank — without having an account number and some form of "identification"!

Biographies are but the clothes and buttons of a person.
The biography of the man himself cannot be written.

-- *Mark Twain (1906)*

8.

Perhaps the most surprising and challenging aspect of this insight was the realization that the natural being that I "really am," does not include a lot of the things that I thought it did. For example, it does not include my legal name, my profession, my accomplishments, my educational degree, my social status or my property ownership. These are important to the well-being of my living self, even essential. But they are among the things in my individual human existence that are not alive. They are created and defined according to the rules of civilized institutions.

These things belong to the non-living rules-based part of myself, not the living part. This is easy to see, because my institutional identity changes as I change institutions. When I switch banks, I get a new account number. When I move to a different state, I apply for a new driver's license. When I take on new employment, I print a new job title on my new business cards. And if I change countries, even my educational degrees may not count. But I am always "Me"!

This all doesn't mean that I should leave the things of my civilized institutional identity behind. Far from it. In fact, I cannot leave them behind. I may be able to change them and improve them – I can move addresses, get a better job, get a new educational degree. And the things of my institutional identity may be "stolen" through "identity theft." But I still cannot do without them. And the reason that I can't do without them, is that they are essential to helping me meet my natural needs in a society made up of institutions.

Too much of the animal distorts the civilized man,
too much civilization makes sick animals.

— *Carl Gustav Jung (1953)*

9.

Our common use of language convinces me that being human is a balance of what is alive and what's not alive. When we identify too much with our institutional roles, non-living rules take over. At this extreme, we may become rigid, cold, robotic; we control others using regulations, position and rank. When we reject institutional rules, our visceral impulses take free rein. At this extreme we may become undisciplined, unpredictable, despotic; we control others using threats, force and violence. We refer to *both* of these states as being "inhuman." To become human again we must return to the balance, where the two forces support and nurture each other. We do this on the one hand through revolt and reassertion of instinctive vitality, and on the other by adopting new institutional rules to restore peace and discipline. Only when the two parts are in balance can we have the unique blend of order, creativity and complex cooperation that we refer to as human civilization.

This interplay of balance and imbalance may lead to the well-known cycles of order and chaos that occur throughout human history. The great civilizations have all risen, flourished and declined. They rise by adopting agreed rules and institutions appropriate to the times. They thrive by supporting the well-being of the living beings that make up the civilization. And they decline when institutions become self-serving and fail to fulfill the natural needs of individual people – so there's no longer enough vitality to support the over-institutionalized framework of civilization, and it crumbles from a lack of life.

In spite of these cycles of order and chaos, this strategy has been wildly successful for our species, because it protects us and provides for our natural needs and well-being better than might be possible in nature alone.

Ideologies and systems have taken the place
of morality and intelligence.

-- attributed to Edward Gibbon,
author of The Decline and Fall
of the Roman Empire (1776)

10.

At some point along the way it occurred to me that this strange system of "being human" has an unexpected effect. One that probably was not intended when we chose to go down the path of agreed rules, institutions and civilization.

The unexpected effect is that the system that makes us human creates a kind of a rift, or fracture, between ourselves as living beings and the natural world at large. Precisely because this strategy takes the place of so many aspects of nature for our own good, it also leaves us with a sense of distance and isolation. We may feel like we were dropped into an alien world, rather than having grown out of it. It may feel like a kind of exile, not only from our natural source, but from each other as well.

In a way this makes sense, because in fact that is what the system is intended to do. Talking-based institutions are meant to come between us and the natural world, to protect us from its dangers. I live and sleep in a house, not in the forest under the stars, buffeted by storms and cold. My house protects me from the dangerous and uncomfortable aspects of nature, but it also stands between me and nature.

Truth be told, it protects me from the dangers of nature precisely *because* it stands between me and nature.

Since the individual entity exists, fictitiously, only
from the outside, being an individual requires
remaining strangers to ourselves.

-- *The Invisible Committee*
NOW (2017)

11.

This sense of distance and isolation also includes a sense of a rift inside each of us – a separation of the living part that participates in the dance of civilization, from the part of our instinctive vitality that's held in check in order for civilization to function. That excluded part of us is always ready to re-emerge, to rebel against the boundaries of institutional rules, to be free from the bonds of – yes – of being human. We feel exiled from nature, separated from each other, and isolated from our own essential source.

We yearn every day to conquer this uncomfortable fracture, this sense of distance and isolation. We long to reconnect with the forgotten source of our natural vitality, however we conceive it. We seek to heal the fracture that makes us human.

He who makes a beast of himself
gets rid of the pain of being a man.

-- *Doctor Johnson (d.1784)*

12.

This sense of fracture and discomfort is with us even when civilization is in its proper balance. Paradoxically, the fracture and discomfort may be at a maximum when there is a balance. This may be one of the reasons that human civilization never seems to manage peaceful stability for very long. Like so many others, I yearn to heal the sense of distance and isolation that I feel even when times are good — this sense of fracture caused by my living self's dependence on words, agreed rules, institutions and institutional identity. I try to soften the hold of the limited persona of civilized life, to feel a deep and direct connection to nature, to other humans, to my own living self. At the same time, I want to feel the security and safety of effective rules that control the unpredictable aspects of human life around me.

We long to bridge this valley, even as we live within the civilization that is the very gift that the valley gives to us. Perhaps *that* is why it's so ding-dang hard to be human: The balance of what's alive and what is not alive in us may be uncomfortable to the point of being unbearable. When our human-ness is at its maximum, our sense of fracture and isolation is also at its maximum. We feel the insecurity and perhaps even anxiety of walking on a razor's edge. We want to move off of this uncomfortable balance to one or the other of the extremes, to vitality, or order. We hope it will be more comforting, and that it will relieve our sense of unease.

But as we move to the extremes, we move farther away from being human. Each extreme is unsustainable, because the other necessary branch of being human will always reassert itself. If we do get to one extreme, we find that it is not what we are looking for. And there are others just waiting in the wings, ready to pull us in the other direction.

What is joy without sorrow?
It's how you look at your suffering,
how you deal with it, that will define you.

-- Mark Twain (c.1906)

13.

And so I realized that the fracture isn't something that keeps us from being human. It is the very thing that makes us human. And the fracture that makes us human, the balance of what is alive and what is not alive, seems unbearable to us.

But our option to move off the balance into a one-sided extreme is no better, since we find each of those extremes to be "inhuman" and unsustainable.

I began to wonder whether we could try to find a way to heal the fracture itself, to ease the discomfort and fear of being human, while remaining on the balance point of being human.

There are some things which cannot be learned quickly. They are the very simplest things, and it takes a person's life to know them.

--*Ernest Hemingway (1932)*

Untalkable Love

We can talk, and
we can love in spite of talking.
It's that simple.

That's what we storytellers do.
We restore order with imagination.
We instill hope again and again and again.

-- attr. Walt Disney (d.1966)

14.

One of the iconic ways that we try to heal the fracture, to bridge the valley between our individual selves and the natural world while remaining characteristically human, is by filling the valley with the products of imagination: art, music, myth, poetry, drama, song, folk tales, parables. In short, with stories. But more often than not, what we are trying to do is this: we are trying to heal the fracture of nature and bring the two parts together into a single whole, while at the same time we want to keep on talking.

I wasn't really sure this is possible, because the very fact of talking and having a word-based identity is what causes the fracture in the first place. Even the tangible expressions of imagination -- art, music, stories — will eventually be subject to agreed rules. They become institutional as soon as they are shared and accepted among us.

Talking to each other and agreed rules make us human, but they create the fracture of life in the process. Our desire to bridge the gap with talking, with our word-based identities, is a desire to be *more* than human, which of course we cannot do at least while we are alive.

If you ask: What are the fruits of silence?
he will say: They are self-control,
true courage or endurance,
patience, dignity, and reverence.

Silence is the cornerstone of character.

-- Ohiyesa, aka Charles A. Eastman
The Soul of the Indian (1911)

Untalkable Love

15.

The next insight I came to was this: Talking to each other, complex cooperation, agreed rules and civilized institutions created the fracture, and they continue to hold it open day by day. But the living self exists without talking; it is our true connection with nature, and with the natural source that we long to find.

Many of us have realized this, and have tried to bridge the gap and reunite with our source by the simple act of stopping talking. Vows of silence, quiet meditation, wordless prayer, zen, even a walk in the beauty of nature, can take us beyond words, and we feel closer to our source. It seemed to me that we were all seeking an aspect of life that is not susceptible to words – that by its very nature cannot be talked about. I came to use an existing dictionary-defined word for this aspect of our everyday reality: "Untalkable - incapable of being talked about."

I thought of untalkable as the essence that unites all people and all of nature. It made sense to me that this is the goal and fascination of religions and philosophies. Just as all roads lead to Rome, all religions and philosophies must point to a single reality. We are all equally human, after all. And since this common reality is by its very nature beyond the ability of words, then each system can use its own words, its own symbols and myths, its own stories and parables. And all of them can point to this single untalkable reality that is the same for everyone.

But words and symbols can only point the way; they cannot embody that reality. Every religion recognizes this in some form, and each one has a tradition of wordlessness. We all recognize that a fundamental part of reality is beyond the reach of words whenever we refer to the "mystery of existence." It is untalkable.

What is honour? A word.
What is in that word honour?
What is that honour?

Air.

-- Shakespeare's Falstaff (1600)

16.

But now I ran into a real problem. I knew that to be human, we are a balanced blend of what is alive, which exists whether or not we use words; and what is not alive, which is created by and dependent on the use of words, of talking to each other, and of agreed rules and complex cooperation. To stop talking also means to stop being human. To put away talking means to undermine the balance of what is alive and what is not alive in us.

But we humans treasure our humanity as much as we long for the peace and wholeness of heaven and nature, and our word-based identity is as indispensable a part of being human as our natural body. We yearn for relief from our suffocating rules, but paradoxically we humans can be freed from our non-living part only when we die.

Truth may be vital
but without love it is unbearable.

-- *Pope Francis (2009)*

Untalkable Love

17.

This seemed to me to border on an impossible dream. And only a miracle can do the impossible. Then I thought a little bit more. I thought about all those that have come before me, and have attested that there is a true miracle in human existence that can indeed do the impossible.

Once I learned that being human is a balance of what is alive and what is not alive in me, and that this creates a fracture between myself and my essential source, I started to wonder whether this state of affairs could be fixed. That is, whether I could remain human, with all its talking to each other and agreed rules and fracture of nature and gap between ourselves and ourselves and so on and so forth, and at the same time heal my sense of separation and isolation from myself, from others, and from nature. In short, whether I could become as whole and comfortable with life as that squirrel and lion, while remaining fully human.

Then it dawned on me that there may be a way we can do the impossible, to bridge the word-based rift in nature while remaining a human that talks. To achieve a sense of connection and belonging at every moment, while continuing to talk to each other and to live in civilization with all its agreed rules, boundaries, cooperation, enforcements and restrictions.

What dawned on me is this: that the magical glue that can heal the fracture is the very thing that we call love. Love connects. It heals. It bridges distance and separation – between different people, between people and their surroundings, even within a single person. It brings us together, it makes us whole.

Love, Beyond All Reason

-- Talby's Fresh Thoughts (2003)

Untalkable Love

18.

This type of love might seem vague, idealistic and impractical. It is not. It is very simple, clear and realistic. The trick is to love in spite of rules. Mothers love their children unconditionally, no matter what rules they break. And the best definition of a friend that I've heard, is someone who will stand by me even when I am in the wrong; that is, even when I break the rules.

This type of love in the face of breaking rules may be the type of love that can bridge the fracture of nature. It can redeem my living self and make me whole in the face of the agreed rules of civilization. Love without rules may be my most direct connection with other living beings and with the natural world.

But we can't live as civilized human beings without rules. In order for civilization to function, we have to have boundaries and guardrails of behavior, complex and sustained cooperation, and enforcement of our agreed rules.

So we must do the impossible: to live by the agreed rules of civilization, while immersing ourselves in love without rules. To continue to talk to each other, and at the same time to embody Untalkable Love.

We grasp our lives in all seriousness
Like a handful of sand in the ocean surf

-- Talby's Fresh Thoughts (2003)

Untalkable Love

19.

What exactly is Untalkable Love? Like so many others, I long to reconnect with my true source. It seems to me that our true source is as a natural living being, directly connected to nature, that does not separate itself from nature with talking. Every human is born such a being, before we encounter words and rules. We begin as a living bundle of Untalkable Love. As we grow, we learn to talk, we learn to abide by the rules, we learn to be a functioning, productive member of institutionalized society, and we become experts at preserving and defending the fracture of life that makes us human. Little by little, we forget what it means to love without words. We forget the Untalkable Love that we were born with.

We forget, because Untalkable Love is separate and apart from the agreed rules of civilization. Love without rules can only mean loving without talking about it. Even using the word love itself creates a fracture. It reduces our understanding of the reality of love to the definition of the word. Words evaluate, limit, constrain. They are not alive. They can name aspects of life, but those aspects of life remain so much more than any words that can point to them.

Untalkable Love is not imaginary. Quite the opposite. It's a direct connection with natural reality, without the intervention of imagination. Words and talking, because they have meaning and are limiting, put a filter of imagination between us and our natural surroundings, a barrier that is as real as the house that we shelter in during a storm. Untalkable Love passes through this barrier to connect us directly to ourselves. Talking and words limit our understanding of love, but love itself is not limited. Yet both of these can exist simultaneously, just as I can hold a bucket of seawater in my hand while standing in the ocean.

Peace of soul can be the gentle radiations of
a rich animality into the moral or religious sphere.

-- *Fred Neechy, aka*
Friedrich Nietzsche (1889)

20.

But my problem still remained. I can't stop talking and still be human. I know this because being human is an interwoven fabric of the part of me that is alive and can exist without talking, and the part that is not alive and requires talking in order to exist. And without either one, I am not human.

To heal the fracture that makes us human, we need to experience love without any rules or limits at all -- to love without words. But how can we do that while remaining human? If being human requires talking to each other, and talking to each other holds open the rift that makes us human every moment of every day, how can I heal this fracture that by its very nature makes me who I am?

Words and imagination do not bridge the gap. They reinforce it and make it deeper and wider. This leads to a seeming contradiction: to experience love without words while still embodying the word-based part of myself.

This is *precisely* the time when artists go to work.
We speak, we write, we do language.
That is how civilizations heal.

-- Toni Morrison (2015)

Untalkable Love

21.

I discovered that I may in fact be able to find Untalkable Love in the sphere of talking to each other, of words, agreed rules, institutions and institutional identity. Untalkable Love, love without words, is a personal direct connection to my natural source. There is no reason that I cannot remain aware of that connection while maintaining the protective civilized barriers that are created with words, talking to each other, agreed rules and sustained cooperation.

It's like welcoming nature inside, after having built the house. Like opening the window and feeling the wind and rain on my face, while still enjoying the safety of the physical structure and the comfort of my home and family.

The artistic individual has let his work
live or die on its own account.
He has never wholly surrendered himself to life.

The creative type who renounces this protection by art to
devote his whole creative force to life and the formation of life
will enjoy, in personality-creation and expression,
a greater happiness.

-- Otto Rank (1932)

Untalkable Love

22.

So if I want to bridge the gap that makes me human, while remaining human, I can bridge it with Untalkable Love. By finding Untalkable Love in the gap, while leaving the gap intact. By feeling Untalkable Love even for the non-living things of institutional civilization – bureaucracy, laws, restrictions and limitations, social success and artistic creations, even my own uncomfortable institutional identity. And for the people that offend my sense of propriety by breaking the rules. I can have Untalkable Love for these as much as I can for my family, nature and the divine.

We can hold to Untalkable Love as we live within the agreed rules of civilization. And we can hold to Untalkable Love when we rebel against unfair and over-restrictive rules and seek change. We can extend Untalkable Love to all the talking-based things that go into making us human and keeping us civilized.

In this sense, Untalkable Love is not love without talking. It is love in spite of talking. Every mother teaches her children to obey rules, while at the same time loving them in spite of all the rules.

We Indians could not conceive of the extremes of luxury
and misery existing side by side in white civilization, for
it was common observation with us that the coarse weeds,
if permitted to grow, will choke out the more delicate flowers.

-- Ohiyesa, From the Deep Woods
to Civilization (1916)

23.

How can Untalkable Love heal the fracture that makes us human? How can it heal my troubling sense of distance and isolation? Untalkable Love may heal these by giving me a new sense of what it means to "heal."

Untalkable Love does not heal the fracture by taking it away. To be fully human I need the balance, and to be balanced I need the fracture. And to accept the fracture, I have to accept its discomfort. Taking away the fracture, just as much as taking away talking, takes away being human. We humans live with an uncomfortable fracture. That's all there is to it.

But while Untalkable Love cannot take away the fracture, it can help make it bearable. Untalkable Love can help me live with the discomfort of being human, instead of trying to push it away and becoming less than human in the process.

So I don't eliminate the fracture with Untalkable Love. Neither do I remove the discomfort of the fracture. But Untalkable Love can help me endure, and even enjoy, both the fracture and its discomfort. Untalkable Love helps me live fully, even when the fracture is at its point of maximum balance, of maximum discomfort, of maximum human-ness.

It's kind of like this: I can live with the discomfort of the fracture that makes me human, by filling the fracture with Untalkable Love. I can walk the razor's edge tightrope of civilized instinct, using a balance-pole of Untalkable Love.

I long, as does every human being,
to be at home wherever I find myself.

-- *Maya Angelou (d.2014)*

Untalkable Love

24.

In a way, Untalkable Love re-defines our sense of distance from life, nature and ourselves. If I feel isolated and in exile, that is only because I think my home is somewhere else. And I think that my home is somewhere else, because I mistakenly believe that my "home" should be comfortable and effortless.

But the truth is that, for now, I am a human being living in nature. There may be other places I could be, and those other places may not have a fracture. They may be effortlessly comfortable. But while I am a human being on this Earth, which means living in a civilized society in the midst of nature, then my home contains the fracture and its sense of discomfort. And all I need to do to feel like I am home, is to realize that this in fact is my home. And then this home may become, one would hope, comfortable and enjoyable, perhaps to the point of delight.

Once I accept this human life as my proper home, and this uncomfortable fracture as the heart of being fully human, then and only then am I truly home. Not effortlessly home, but still home.

The point of human balance is not a place of rest. Aristotle defined Soul as "being at work staying itself." He believed that once something discovers its true essence, it wants to remain there. It wants to "stay itself." But staying itself is not automatic. It requires effort. It requires work. Soul is not effortless.

Some things may be effortless, but being fully human is not one of them.

Wisdom is brain in the service of heart

-- *Talby's Fresh Thoughts (2003)*

Untalkable Love

25.

We can heal the fracture that makes us human, while remaining balanced and fully human, by letting civilization be civilization and adding Untalkable Love. Hold the institutional identity to its proper purpose of serving the well-being of the living self. Let the agreed rules of civilization play their role because civilization without rules is impossible. Enforce the rules when they need enforcing. Change the rules when they need changing. But hold to Untalkable Love while doing so.

Not to love in the absence of rules. But to let the rules be, and experience Untalkable Love in spite of the rules. We can play by the rules without being ruled by them, if we let the rules apply to everything but love. We can talk, *and* we can love in spite of talking.

It's that simple.

This is what you shall do: Love the earth and sun and the animals, despise riches, give alms to every one that asks, stand up for the stupid and crazy, devote your income and labor to others, hate tyrants, argue not concerning God, have patience and indulgence toward the people, take off your hat to nothing known or unknown or to any man or number of men, go freely with powerful uneducated persons and with the young and with the mothers of families, read these leaves in the open air every season of every year of your life, re-examine all you have been told at school or church or in any book, dismiss whatever insults your own soul, and your very flesh shall be a great poem and have the richest fluency not only in its words but in the silent lines of its lips and face and between the lashes of your eyes and in every motion and joint of your body.

-- *Walt Whitman (1885)*

Untalkable Love

This is the magic of Untalkable Love.

To heal the human fracture that is the result of talking,

while still talking,

by adding Untalkable Love.

God save the foundation.

-- Shakespeare's Dogberry (1612)

Untalkable Love

Some Additional Words

Render unto Caesar the things that are Caesar's,
And render unto God the things that are God's.

-- Gospel of St. Mark

Untalkable Love

Personal Manifesto

I believe that we humans are a balance of what is alive and what is not alive in us. And what is not alive in us arises from our ability to talk to each other, to echo nature in words and grammar, in order to achieve complex cooperation through agreed rules, and to create the institutions of society, and ourselves as mini-institutions with an institutional identity.

I believe that this state of affairs which makes us human causes a fracture within ourselves, as well as a fracture in society, and in nature itself. I further believe that one way we can heal this fracture is by finding and accepting Untalkable Love while living our human life in a civilized and talking society. To find Untalkable Love in our talking, our rules, our institutions, our own institutional identity, for the service they provide to our Living Self.

We can discover for ourselves the reality of love without words, and we can embrace this Untalkable Love while living a talking human life. This is the strategy we can use to remain human and keep on talking to each other, while at the same time transcending the fracture of life by loving in spite of rules, in spite of words, in spite of talking. To be able to do this, we only need to recognize the civilized limits of talking, and the reality of Untalkable Love that is beyond it.

This is a simple and practical path to healing the fracture that makes us human. Once we find this, we are home – in our uniquely human home. We can heal the rift of human existence while remaining human, through a combination and balance of talking to each other, plus Untalkable Love.

The first man who flung a word of abuse
at his enemy instead of a spear
was the founder of civilization.

-- *Sigmund Freud (1893)*

Untalkable Love

Flow: An Overview

Civilization is made up of living beings plus institutions.

Institutions are made up of living beings plus agreed rules.

Agreed rules are made up by people who can talk to each other.

Talking to each other is made possible because we humans are living beings who can sound an unlimited number of words arranged according to the grammar of the natural world.

Each human being is a balanced blend of a living self with instinctive vitality, which can exist without words, and a rules-based institutional identity, which requires words to exist.

Living beings are alive. Agreed rules are not alive, but they have a profound effect on living beings. This alchemy of what is alive in us, plus what is not alive in us, makes possible the complex and stable cooperation necessary for civilization to exist. But only the living self has natural feelings, needs and well-being. The institutional identity exists to serve these.

Civilization is created by living beings as a woven fabric of natural instinctive vitality plus word-based institutional rules. These must be in balance for civilization to thrive. When they are out of balance, the fabric of civilization begins to unravel. The tension and flow between these two forces creates the cycles of order and chaos throughout the history of human civilization.

An artifact of this system, is that it creates a fracture, a rift, a gap. Between civilized humans and nature. Between people and other people. And even within our individual selves. We cannot remove this gap and remain human, because being human requires talking and institutional identity, which are the very things that create the gap. But the gap causes us to feel alienated and alone. We long to heal this fracture, the fracture that makes us human.

The only way to heal the fracture while remaining human, is to keep on talking to each other and operating within agreed rules, while at the same time feeling and expressing healing, connecting love. Love without words. Love in spite of rules. To love without talking, while keeping on talking. Untalkable love.

Sign, sign, everywhere a sign
Blockin' out the scenery, breakin' my mind
Do this, don't do that, can't you read the sign?

-- Five Man Electrical Band
"Signs" (1971)

Untalkable Love

Unbearable Balance

The point of balance between what is alive in us and what is not alive in us, is the point of maximum "human-ness." But it is also, for the same reasons, the point of our maximum fracture. It is highly uncomfortable, perhaps to the point of being unbearable.

This may explain why, throughout history, we have been incapable of maintaining the balance point which keeps us human, peaceful and cooperative. We feel so uncomfortable with the sense of fracture and alienation from nature and from ourselves, that we long to push away from it to something more comfortable. Half of us push toward instinctive freeing unruly vitality, half of us push toward more effective orderly restrictive rules. The two sides demonize each other, blaming each other for the discomfort.

Eventually one side wins, society careens toward one extreme, and the balanced fabric of society seems to unravel before our eyes. Then, just as suddenly, the other side reacts and swings us back to the other extreme. Eventually everyone is exhausted and we return to the middle –

To the balance point of being human.

To the point of maximum fracture, of maximum discomfort, of maximum human-ness.

And then it starts all over.....

The solution is Untalkable Love

"Truth is vital, but without love it can be unbearable."

Who have hills and valleys in their chest
can live in a city as in a mountain wood

-- Zhang Chao (c.1685)

Untalkable Love

What we want to be, is this: We want to heal the fracture of Nature and bring the two parts together into one, while at the same time we want to keep on talking, thinking, having an identity, and being civilized.

I'm not really sure this is possible, because the very fact of talking and having an "identity" is what causes the fracture of nature in the first place. We tend to look to Spirit, to divinity, to poetry, to stories, to bridge this gap. To fill it up with something that fixes the fracture while at the same time containing words. I believe this futile quest is the origin of religion, rather than direct experience and knowledge of nature, creation, of the source of that creation, and it is also the origin of the myriad wonderful manifestations of human imagination which include art literature science and yes even madness.

The magical glue that can do this is the thing that we call love. But I firmly believe it is Love without words. Love Without Words is the only unconditional kind of love that there is. Once there's even a single word, love is no longer unconditional. It is subject to the rules of that word.

So my belief is that the only way to heal the fracture of nature, which also reflects as a fracture inside of ourselves, is love without words. The word love itself creates a fracture in life. So we must discover the reality of love without even the word love.

Untalkable Love is so much more then could ever be described by the word love. It is an aspect of reality, pure reality. And the words we put on it can only limit it, including the very word love. Without any words we can have a direct experience of nature. Without any words we can have a direct experience of wholeness. Without any words we can have a direct experience of love.

Connecting to the other side of the gap. The connection has to be without words. The part of me on the other side of the gap is fully immersed in nature. And connecting with it connects me directly to Nature. But only without words. Who was it that first said the highest form of Consciousness is awareness without analysis?

We're all longing to return to our true source. I believe our true source is as a natural living being, directly connected to Nature, that does not talk. Once we find this, we are home. Whether it's through death, or finding the connection during our civilized life. We are home.

Only when we have made ourselves at home in a solid
'theory of things' capable of supporting civilization
can we bring our magnificent ideals into effective agreement
with reality. It is from new ideas that we build history anew.

-- *para. Albert Schweitzer*
Philosophy of Civilization (1923)

Untalkable Love

Contact
kaerlud-301@yahoo.com

www.ingramcontent.com/pod-product-compliance
Lightning Source LLC
Chambersburg PA
CBHW080527030426
42337CB00023B/4657